The Great Chicago Fire

Written by Tria Smith
Illustrated by Shawn Stucky

MEDIA ENHANCED BOOKS
AV2 BY WEIGL™
ADDED VALUE • AUDIO VISUAL
www.av2books.com

In partnership with redmoon

This is a special media enhanced book. With the codes below, you have full access to video, audio, weblinks, and activities. You also receive a readalong eBook that will read to you or allow you to read on your own.

Go to **www.av2books.com**, and enter this book's unique code.

BOOK CODE

W 5 8 4 5 3 3

AV² by **Weigl** brings you media enhanced books that support active learning.

AV² Readalong Navigation

HIGHLIGHTED TEXT

HOME 🏠

CLOSE ⊗

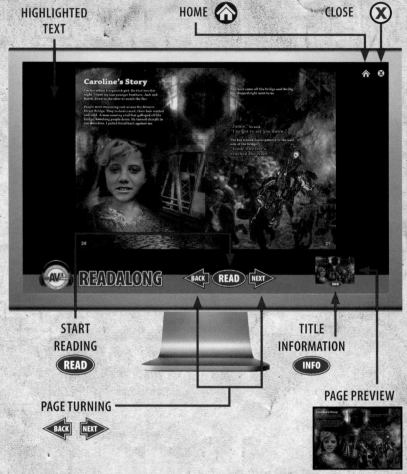

START READING
READ

PAGE TURNING
BACK NEXT

TITLE INFORMATION
INFO

PAGE PREVIEW

Go to **www.av2books.com**, and enter this book's unique code.

BOOK CODE

S 7 3 5 8 9 6

Your AV² media enhanced books come alive with...

Audio
Listen to sections of the book read aloud.

Key Words
Study vocabulary, and complete a matching word activity.

Video
Watch informative video clips.

Quizzes
Test your knowledge.

Embedded Weblinks
Gain additional information for research.

Slide Show
View images and captions, and prepare a presentation.

Try This!
Complete activities and hands-on experiments.

... and much, much more!

The Great Chicago Fire

The Great Chicago Fire Festival

The Great Chicago Fire Festival is a citywide event. It was created to unite neighborhoods of Chicago and show the world its strength through an intergenerational event, celebrating Chicago's epic resurgence following the fire of 1871.

In partnership with AV² by Weigl, Redmoon has worked with a team of curriculum experts and artists to create this book. Our goals are to engage youth in a story that champions the Great Chicago Fire Festival's themes of grit and resilience, and to inspire them to see everyday examples of strength.

Throughout the summer of 2014, neighborhoods across Chicago have gathered to share their stories of resilience and celebration. On October 4th, along the main branch of the Chicago River, people from around Chicago and the world will come together to take part in a larger-than-life Spectacle like no other. Sculptures will burn atop huge floats. Live music will echo deep into the night sky. There will be food, sounds of laughter, love, and astonishment. With the Great Chicago Fire Festival, our magnificent city will continue to amaze and flourish, forever gaining strength from the ashes.

Visit **www.redmoon.org** or call **312-850-8440** for more information.

Major Sponsors

This book is made possible through the generous support of
David and Suzu Neithercut.

Redmoon gratefully acknowledges Linda Weigl for inspiring
The Great Chicago Fire book. Our thanks to AV² by Weigl for publishing
and printing the book, and for creating the AV² Fiction Readalong
and media enhanced online content.

Map of Chicago 1871

Store
Harrison and Canal

O'Leary House
Taylor and Jefferson

Conley's Patch

WHAT IS THE ROUTE?

As you read the story, you will discover we travel far to reach the lake.

Trace their steps.

Draw on this map. Use the landmarks to map the journey.

Monroe Street Bridge

Armory
Market and Jackson

Beach
Monroe Street

Water Tower
The firemen's hose went limp because the Chicago Waterworks building burned. The building was made from sandstone, but the roof was a combination of wood and tar. The ceiling collapsed, damaging the pumps below.

LAKE MICHIGAN

Mrs. O'Leary's Story

You all know me, don't you? It was my doing.
My cow. My lantern. My barn. I let it happen.
Is that what you think?

And what kind of sensible woman sets her
lantern in the hay near a beast's foot?
Now that would be foolish.

They say I did that. Me, who's milked cows
since I could walk.
It's true, though. The Chicago Fire did start
on my street, on Dekoven Street on
October 8, 1871.

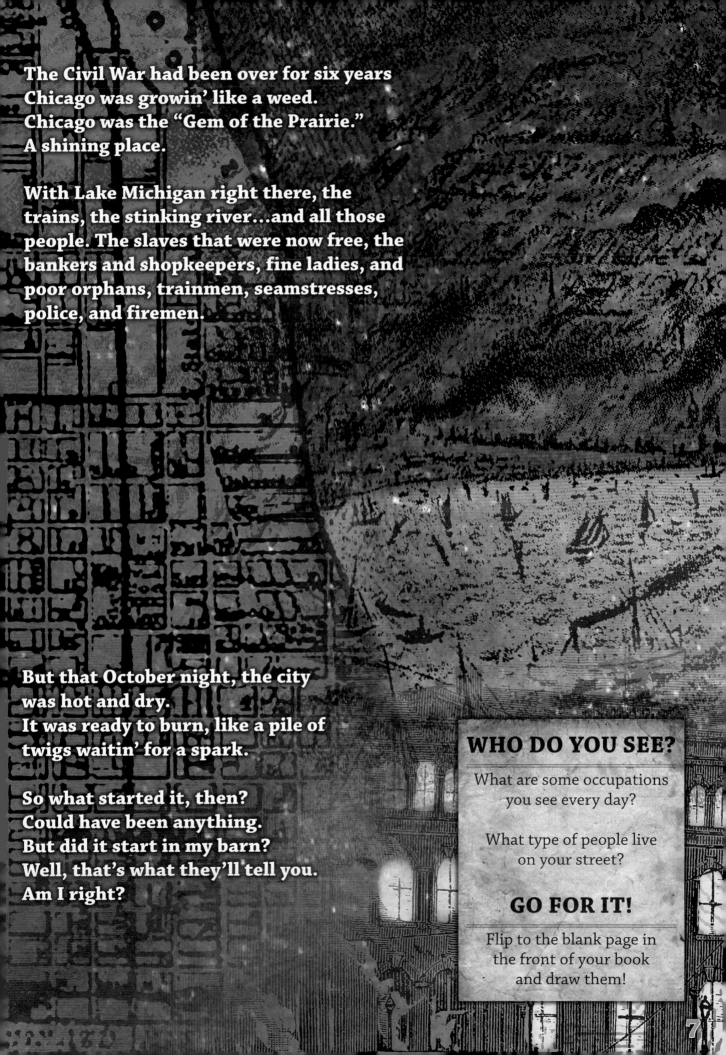

The Civil War had been over for six years
Chicago was growin' like a weed.
Chicago was the "Gem of the Prairie."
A shining place.

With Lake Michigan right there, the
trains, the stinking river…and all those
people. The slaves that were now free, the
bankers and shopkeepers, fine ladies, and
poor orphans, trainmen, seamstresses,
police, and firemen.

But that October night, the city
was hot and dry.
It was ready to burn, like a pile of
twigs waitin' for a spark.

So what started it, then?
Could have been anything.
But did it start in my barn?
Well, that's what they'll tell you.
Am I right?

WHO DO YOU SEE?

What are some occupations
you see every day?

What type of people live
on your street?

GO FOR IT!

Flip to the blank page in
the front of your book
and draw them!

Nate's Story

This is the story of how I met Caroline and her brothers the night of the Great Fire, how we buried treasure together, and how a melted pocket watch made all the difference.

My momma died on our train trip up to Chicago. After that, Mr. and Mrs. Kirk took me in. I helped tend their shop.

The Kirks fed me. They gave me a place to sleep and I did what I could to help. I swept, made towers of cans, neatly lined up the shoes, and cared for the animals.

I played with their son Jamie, who was five. I watched him when his parents went out. I cooked, too. I made Jamie cabbage and ham, baked apples, and sweet milk.

It was Sunday night around 9:30, and the Kirks were at the Methodist church, singing. I was wrapped in my quilt, dreaming, when someone banged wildly upon the front door.

"Fire!" he shouted.

"You need to get out!!"

I sat straight up.

Jamie ran to the
bedroom window.
A block away, a
giant wave of flames
rose up and broke
over the rooftops.
Afraid, Jamie dove
under the bed.
I didn't know
what to do.

Should we wait for the Kirks to
return? No, we needed to get
somewhere safe.

I threw on my clothes and
reached for my shoes.

I laced my shoes tight and crawled under the bed to get Jamie.

"I'm not leaving," he said.

"Momma will find me if I stay here. Not going, not going..."

I had to do this right. I pulled him out and onto my lap. I held him tight and spoke quietly.

"Now there are some big fireworks going off, and we want to get to a special spot to watch. We need a really good view. Okay?"

Jamie's body relaxed. He looked up at me.

"Yeah?"

"I'm going to get you there. Don't let go of my hand," I said. "Lots of other people are trying to get there, too."

Flames pushed up against the glass window we'd stood at just moments before. I was tying Jamie's shoe when the glass broke, and the fire reached in like a hand and touched the bed. We ran.

THINK ABOUT A TIME YOU WERE BRAVE

How did you find your courage?

The front door was locked. My hand shook so badly, I couldn't even get the key in the lock. Inside my head, I commanded myself in a great voice: "You can do this. Unlock the door."

I looked back at the animals in their cages. The birds. My favorite green parrot.

I said, "Jamie, let the dogs and cats free. I'll get the birds."

In a flash we undid the cage doors. This was a kind of dream come true; to free the animals. But the birds wouldn't leave. I lunged at them and rattled their cages.

"Go! Go!"

Outside, everyone seemed to be carrying some sort of burden. Giant bundles wrapped in quilts and sheets. Candelabras, mirrors, paintings, musical instruments.

"Look. Red Snow!" Jamie shouted.

Shining, drifting flakes made everything
suddenly feel very slow. The world became
silent. I saw the green parrot struggle to
fly through the burning sky.

Suddenly, nearby, a horse reared, jolting us from our awe. I turned to Jamie and our eyes met.

"Fireworks!" I said.

"Fireworks!" Jamie repeated.

We grasped hands and ran.

People shouted as they crossed each other's paths. The ash became so thick it struck our faces and sank into our clothing. One hot coal the size of a half-dollar hit my arm. My shirt began to flame, but a woman beside me quickly slapped it out.

Two men carried a very old man on a wooden door.

A woman kneeled in the middle of the street, praying. Her skirt was burning.

We saw firemen working together, aiming their hose at a burning building. The water boiled when it hit the flames, then turned to steam. Then, without warning, the hose went limp and the water trickled to nothing.
The firefighters held it in amazement.

"There's no water!"
one of them shouted.

WATER BOILS AND TURNS TO STEAM

Look it up. At what temperature does water boil?

We came to the Monroe Street Bridge, overloaded with a crush of people trying to get across. We were all packed together so tightly, the crowd practically carried Jamie and me along. Then, Jamie was pulled away from me. I bent down and peered through the trudging legs. I grasped Jamie by his white nightshirt.

I lifted him up to sit on top of my shoulders so he could see. He quickly slid down and wrapped his legs around my waist.

"Up high is scary," he said.

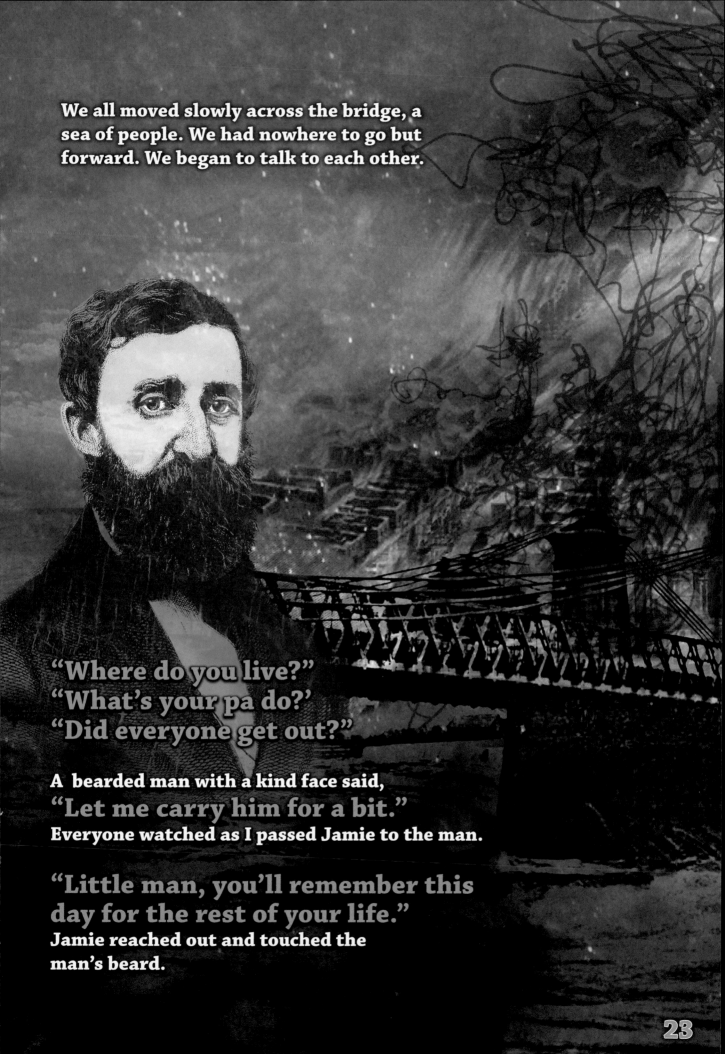

We all moved slowly across the bridge, a sea of people. We had nowhere to go but forward. We began to talk to each other.

"Where do you live?"
"What's your pa do?"
"Did everyone get out?"

A bearded man with a kind face said,
"Let me carry him for a bit."
Everyone watched as I passed Jamie to the man.

"Little man, you'll remember this day for the rest of your life."
Jamie reached out and touched the man's beard.

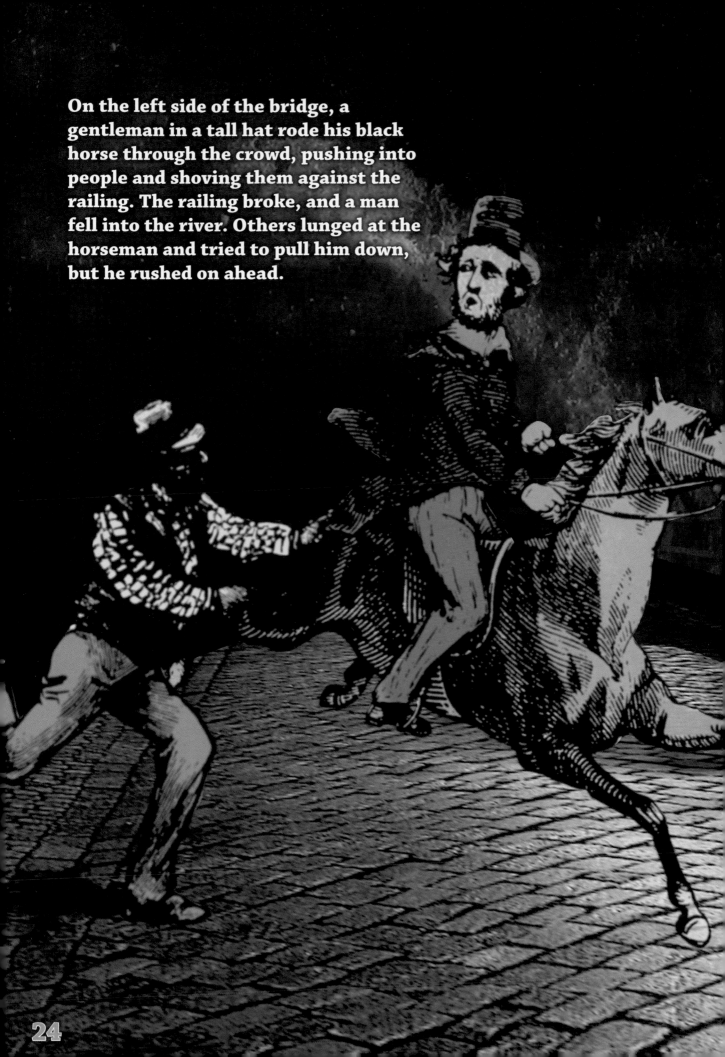

On the left side of the bridge, a gentleman in a tall hat rode his black horse through the crowd, pushing into people and shoving them against the railing. The railing broke, and a man fell into the river. Others lunged at the horseman and tried to pull him down, but he rushed on ahead.

Caroline's Story

I'm the oldest Fitzpatrick girl. On that terrible night, I took my two younger brothers, Jack and David, down to the river to watch the fire.

People were streaming east across the Monroe Street Bridge. They looked crazed, their hair matted and wild. A man wearing a tall hat galloped off the bridge, knocking people down. He turned sharply in our direction. I pulled David back against me.

Two boys came off the bridge and the big boy stopped right next to us.

"Jamie," he said, "I've got to set you down."

The boy named Jamie pointed to the west side of the bridge, "Look! The fire's reached the river."

"The river will stop the fire," said Jack, who was a year younger than I. David, the youngest, leaned toward Jamie. "It'll never get across," he agreed.

Just then, a column of flame twisted in the wind. It hurled itself from one rooftop to another, like a beast of fire. I willed it to stay in its place, to not cross the river. But it did. With terrific force, the flames leapt from the burning buildings on one side of the river and swept across to the other. We saw a white shirt sail through the air. Tossed and twisted by flames, its shirtsleeves stretched out, blazing...

CAN YOU IMAGINE?

What do you think a beast of fire looks like?

DRAW IT HERE.

Add words that describe what it would sound, smell, and feel like.

That's when I knew we had to run.
"We must get Momma!" I shouted. We knew
how to run. Our feet were bare, but they were fast.

"Come with us!" I yelled over my shoulder, and
the two boys followed us.

We turned in at Wells and Monroe and burst into our
Momma's shack.

A lot of houses were packed tight into that area.

People called it "Conley's Patch",
and we didn't care one bit.

"The fire's crossed the river!"
"We got to go."

Momma and I packed our trunk fast. There was no doubt that the sewing machine was the most important item. She and I had saved for it, and we had just begun to make a little money sewing dresses and linens.

With the sewing machine,
we could earn a living no
matter where we lived.

Outside, we heard an awful burst of explosions. Jack and I laid the trunk in a baby carriage and David grabbed our hen.

Nate said "Jamie, help me carry these blankets."

We had a long walk before we would reach the lake.

DRAW YOUR NEIGHBORHOOD

Flip to the blank page in the front of your book. Draw a map.

How do landmarks contribute to your neighborhood?

Draw three landmarks that are important to you.

Out on the street, people shouted news.

"Sherman house is going."

"The opera house caught fire."

"The bridges are burning."

"All escape is cut off to the south and west."

A man stood on a piano, crying out, "Fire is the friend of the poor man!"

Another man held a flame to a pile of costly furniture until it caught fire.

Flames poured in from a side street with the force of a blowtorch. The song of the fire had many sounds within it.

Great dry bundles of twigs snapping and breaking. Squirrels skittering up the sides of trees, their claws clicking on the bark. High wind through dry leaves. Other sounds too, like thousands of hands clapping, waves crashing, a deep growling, and even deeper inside, the high-pitched notes, like a tea kettle, a train whistle's mournful cry, a woman singing.

When we finally got to the lake, we dropped everything and waded into the water. My clothes floated away from my body. We scooped up water and poured it into our mouths.

I lay back and floated. My hair drifted away from my head. There was a kind of silence and a hollow roar under the water. I looked up at the sky and felt so grateful, so lucky.

WHAT CAN YOU HEAR?

Plug your ears. What *can't* you hear anymore?

Shhh...
Whisper yourself a message!

When I stood, I could see the fire getting closer.
We rushed to the shore.

People's belongings were scattered all over the sand.
Boxes, safes, and carts. Books, toys,
and mattresses. Bolts of fabric.

I thought, *Nothing but the lake
is going to stop this fire.*

"We have to bury the trunk," I yelled.

"David, Jamie, go collect sticks."
They went and the other boys followed.

Pretty soon, other children came, offering to help. We worked and worked, and I was in charge.

"A little deeper on that side there," I said.

"We have to go even further down."

The children dug with all their might.

By the time we were ready to bury the trunk, ten children had gathered. We lifted it together and set it in the hole. Each child pushed sand into the hole until we had built it into a mound.

HOW FAST CAN YOU DIG A HOLE WITH A STICK?

Try it. Time yourself.

How much faster could you dig if you had help?

The fire had reached the beach. I watched the fire devour our baby carriage. We had to turn our backs to the flames because its heat burned our noses, our eyes, and the insides of our mouths. There was nowhere for us to go but back into the lake. We dropped down into the water to get away from the heat. I watched as the fire burned itself out at the water's edge. It had eaten everything on the shore and when there was nothing more to eat, it died.

When it was all over, we lay where the water met the shore, waiting for the beach to cool. Our mound was still there. The fire hadn't gotten it. We uncovered the trunk and lifted it. Running all around us, our hen seemed happy.

The boys wandered off and came back with things that had burnt: a brass candlestick all twisted out of shape, a glass bottle bent in half, fused nails. The boys made a small stack of burnt objects they'd collected.

TRUNK SAVED!

Why do you think burying the trunk saved it from the fire?

With our collection we built
a house, a church, a fire
station, a store...

A couple in a carriage rode along the shore. The woman called out to Nate.

"Excuse me, what's that you're holding?"

"Looks to me like a melted pocket watch, ma'am."
Nate held it up for her to see.

"How much do you want for it?"

"Jamie, how much do you think it should cost?"

"A dollar."

"I'll take it,"
the woman said.

"Yes, ma'am."
Nate handed it up to her.

"What a wonderful relic of the fire."

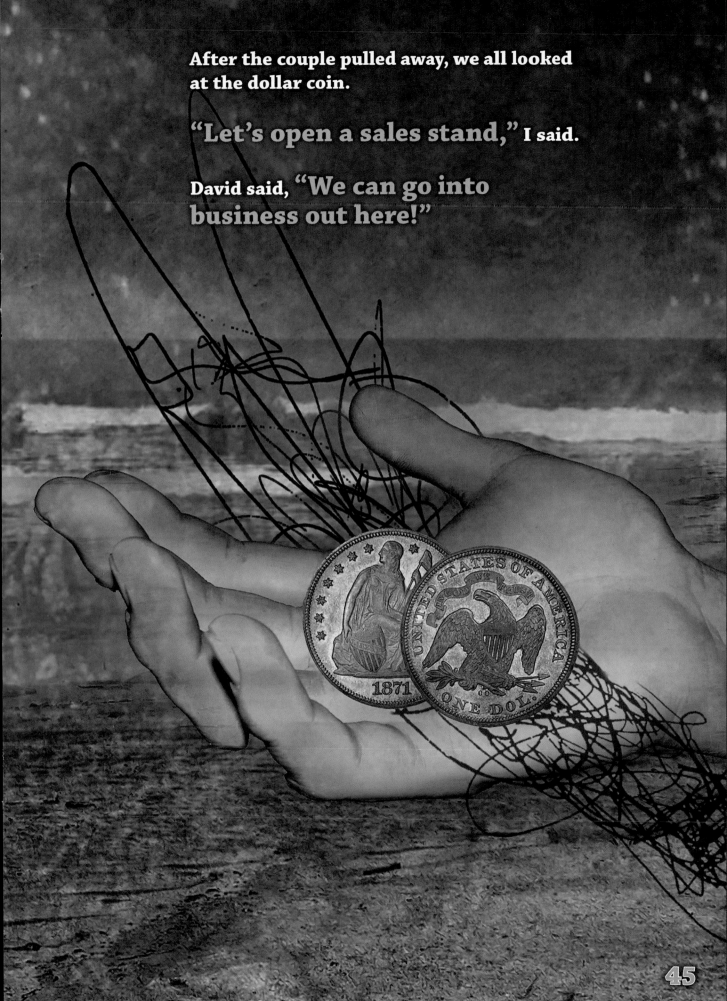

After the couple pulled away, we all looked at the dollar coin.

"Let's open a sales stand," I said.

David said, "We can go into business out here!"

Mrs. O'Leary

And that's just what children all over the city did. They searched the ruins, unearthing melted marbles, burnt teapots, coins in clumps, porcelain doll pieces, ivory billiard balls, even twisted silverware. They sold it all for money.

There it was, the spirit of Chicago, that pushes us to keep on going, to start again, to rise from the ashes like a great bird.

"SPIRIT OF CHICAGO?"

What is Mrs. O'Leary referring to?

Think about a time when you were resilient.

Flip to the blank page in the back of your book. Write one challenge for your neighborhood to overcome and one message of celebration.

The city of Chicago did rise again. Folks hauled the wreckage from the burned city to the lake. That debris made new land. Millennium Park, the Art Institute of Chicago, and Buckingham Fountain all sit on debris from the Great Chicago Fire. Next time you dig at the beach, if you dig deep enough, you might try to find a relic of your own.

Fifty years later, a newspaper man admitted he had made up the tale about my cow starting the fire. He thought it would make a good story. Of course, it did. But it's almost as hard to stop a good story as it is a great fire.

Special Thanks: Jim Lasko, Frank Maugeri, Sophia Wong Boccio, Emily Reusswig, Rebecca Rugg, Dee Dee Pacheco, Angela Tillges, Dr. Barbara Radner, Marcelo Caplan, Mario Rossero, Cynthia Slater-Green, Martin Moe, Kevin Rieg, Michael Manning, Affinity Table Thinkers, Redmoon Staff, Emily Sautter, Kylia Kummer, Jessica Thebus, Samantha Handel, and Sonia Soler.

Redmoon wishes to thank our board and donors listed below that helped support this project.

Published by AV² by Weigl
350 5ᵗʰ Avenue, 59ᵗʰ Floor
New York, NY 10118
Websites: www.av2books.com   www.weigl.com

ISBN 978-1-4896-1930-3 (hardcover)
ISBN 978-1-4896-1932-7 (single-user eBook)
ISBN 978-1-4896-1933-4 (multi-user eBook)

Printed in the United States of America in North Mankato, Minnesota
1 2 3 4 5 6 7 8 9 0 18 17 16 15 14

072014
WEP210714

Project Coordinator: Katie Gillespie
Senior Editor: Heather Kissock
Art Director: Terry Paulhus
Editor: Pamela Dell
Editor: Jillian Gryzlak
Activity Designer: Cynthia Castiglione